COOL
Sausage Recipes

Main Dishes for Beginning Chefs

Alex Kuskowski

Checkerboard Library

An Imprint of Abdo Publishing
abdopublishing.com

abdopublishing.com

Published by Abdo Publishing, a division of ABDO, PO Box 398166, Minneapolis, Minnesota 55439. Copyright © 2017 by Abdo Consulting Group, Inc. International copyrights reserved in all countries. No part of this book may be reproduced in any form without written permission from the publisher. Checkerboard Library™ is a trademark and logo of Abdo Publishing.

Printed in the United States of America,
North Mankato, Minnesota
102016
012017

THIS BOOK CONTAINS RECYCLED MATERIALS

Design and Production: Mighty Media, Inc.
Series Editor: Liz Salzmann
Photo Credits: Mighty Media, Inc.; Shutterstock

The following manufacturers/names appearing in this book are trademarks: Oster®, Pepperidge Farm®, Pyrex®

Publisher's Cataloging-in-Publication Data

Names: Kuskowski, Alex, author.
Title: Cool sausage recipes: main dishes for beginning chefs / by Alex Kuskowski.
Other titles: Main dishes for beginning chefs
Description: Minneapolis, MN : Abdo Publishing, 2017. I Series: Cool main dish recipes I Includes bibliographical references and index.
Identifiers: LCCN 2016944824 I ISBN 9781680781366 (lib. bdg.) I ISBN 9781680775563 (ebook)
Subjects: LCSH: Cooking--Juvenile literature. I Dinners and dining--Juvenile literature. I Entrees (Cooking)--Juvenile literature. I One-dish meals--Juvenile literature.
Classification: DDC 641.82--dc23
LC record available at http://lccn.loc.gov/2016944824

TO ADULT HELPERS

Get cooking! This is your chance to help a budding chef. Being able to cook meals is a life skill. Learning to cook gives kids new experiences and helps them gain confidence. These recipes are designed to help kids learn how to cook on their own. They may need more assistance on some recipes than others. Be there to offer guidance when they need it. Encourage them to do as much as they can on their own. Make sure to have rules for cleanup. There should always be adult supervision when kids are using sharp utensils or a hot oven or stove.

SAFETY FIRST!

Some recipes call for activities or ingredients that require caution. If you see these symbols, ask an adult for help.

HOT STUFF!
This recipe requires the use of a stove or oven. Always use pot holders when handling hot objects.

SUPER SHARP!
This recipe includes the use of a sharp utensil, such as a knife or grater.

NUT ALERT!
Some people can get very sick if they eat nuts. If you cook something with nuts, let people know!

Contents

Super-Duper Sausage!

The main dish is where you start when planning a meal. It's the most important part. Then you choose salads, side dishes, and **desserts** to go with the main dish. Sausage is a great base for many main dishes. It is a favorite meat of people all over the world. It's easy to make, tasty to eat, and there are tons of ways to prepare it!

There are many kinds of sausage and many ways to cook it. Fry up a sweet blueberry breakfast sausage. Make a tasty sausage **gyro**. Chow down on an apple sausage salad.

Try all of the sausage recipes in this book. Then think of your own ways to cook sausage. The possibilities are endless!

I ♥ SAUSAGE

What's not to love about sausage?

Sausage is ground meat stuffed in a casing. Pork, beef, chicken, and turkey can all be used to make sausage. Find out how to pick the best sausage for your recipes.

FRESH SAUSAGE is made from fresh meat. It must be cooked thoroughly before eating it. Italian **pork** sausage, breakfast sausage, and bratwurst are some fresh sausages.

SMOKED SAUSAGE is preserved with smoke from a wood fire. Kielbasa is one of the most popular kinds.

COOKED SAUSAGE is made with fresh meat and then fully cooked. Common cooked sausages include hot dogs and liver sausage.

DRY SAUSAGE keeps for a long time and is often eaten cold. Salami and summer sausage are kinds of dry sausage.

HANDLING THE MEAT

Thaw any frozen sausage in a bowl filled with water. Wash thawed sausage under running water. Pat it dry with a **towel**.

KEEP IT CLEAN

Wash your hands before and after touching the meat. Wash any **utensils** that touched raw meat separately from other dishes.

STORING THE MEAT

Most sausage needs to be stored in the refrigerator. If it does, the label will say "keep refrigerated."

COOKING THE MEAT

Fresh sausage and some smoked sausage must be cooked before you can eat it. Cook the sausage until there is no pink left. Pink meat or juice means the sausage is uncooked.

COOKING BASICS

Ask Permission

- Before you cook, ask **permission** to use the kitchen, cooking tools, and ingredients.

- If you'd like to do something yourself, say so! Just remember to be safe.

- If you would like help, ask for it!

Be Prepared

- Be organized. Knowing where everything is makes cooking safer and more fun!

- Read the directions all the way through before starting a recipe. Follow the directions in order.

- The most important ingredient is preparation! Make sure you have everything you'll need.

Be Smart, Be Safe

- 🐄 Never cook if you are home alone.

- 🐄 Always have an adult nearby for hot jobs, such as using the oven or the stove.

- 🐄 Have an adult around when using a sharp tool, such as a knife or a grater. Always be careful when using these tools!

- 🐄 Remember to turn pot handles toward the back of the stove. That way you won't accidentally knock the pots over.

Be Neat, Be Clean

- 🐓 Start with clean hands, clean tools, and a clean work surface.

- 🐓 Tie back long hair to keep it out of the food.

- 🐓 Wear comfortable clothing and roll up your sleeves.

- 🐓 Put extra ingredients and tools away when you're done.

- 🐓 Wash all the dishes and **utensils**. Clean up your workspace.

COOKING TERMS

BEAT

Beat means to mix well using a whisk or electric mixer.

DICE

Dice means to cut something into small squares.

DRAIN

Drain means to remove liquid using a colander or the pot lid.

SLICE

Slice means to cut something into pieces of the same thickness.

SPRINKLE

Sprinkle means to drop small pieces of something.

BOIL

Boil means to heat liquid until it begins to bubble.

CHOP

Chop means to cut something into small pieces.

MINCE

Mince means to cut or chop something into very tiny pieces.

SIMMER

Simmer means to cook something so it bubbles gently.

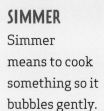

STIR

Stir means to mix ingredients together, usually with a large spoon.

WHISK

Whisk means to beat quickly by hand with a whisk or a fork.

INGREDIENTS

Here are some of the ingredients you will need.

bell peppers

blueberries

cucumber

feta cheese

garlic

Greek yogurt

mixed greens

mustard

penne pasta

pine nuts

sausages, variety

spinach leaves

thyme

tomatoes

broccoli florets

carrots

cayenne pepper

cherry tomatoes

green beans

honey

lemon juice

maple syrup

pita rounds

premade puff pastry

red onion

sage

walnuts

white beans

white onion

zucchini

TOOLS

Here are some of the tools you will need.

aluminum foil

baking sheet

forks

frying pan

large pot

mixing spoon

rubber spatula

saucepan

basting brush

colander

cutting board

measuring cups

measuring spoons

mixing bowls

sharp knife

spatula

whisk

BLUEBERRY
Breakfast Sausage

Break into a tasty breakfast!

1 pound ground pork
  sausage
½ cup blueberries, cut in
  half
1 teaspoon salt
1 teaspoon black pepper
1 tablespoon sage

1 tablespoon thyme
3 tablespoons maple syrup

measuring cups
sharp knife
cutting board
measuring spoons
mixing bowl
frying pan
spatula
pot holders

1 Put all the ingredients except the syrup in a bowl. Mix with your hands.

2 Roll the mixture into 1½-inch (4 cm) balls. Flatten the balls into **patties**.

3 Put several patties in the frying pan over medium heat. Cook for 5 minutes or until there is no more pink. Turn the patties over every few minutes. Repeat until all of the patties are cooked.

4 Add the syrup. Turn the heat to medium-high. Simmer for 30 seconds. Flip the patties over. Simmer for 30 more seconds. Take the patties out of the pan.

1

2

3

PORK
Sausage Rolls

Roll up a tasty surprise!

INGREDIENTS

2 sheets premade puff
  pastry
4 tablespoons mustard
8 pork sausages
1 egg, beaten

TOOLS

measuring spoons
small bowl
whisk
baking sheet
aluminum foil
sharp knife
cutting board
basting brush
pot holders

1. Preheat the oven to 350 degrees. Cover the baking sheet with aluminum foil.

2. Cut each puff pastry sheet in half **diagonally**. Brush mustard on top of each pastry.

3. Roll each pastry around a sausage. Pinch the edges of the pastry closed.

4. Place the rolls on the baking sheet. Brush the outside of each one with egg.

5. Bake for 15 minutes, or until the pastry is golden brown.

2

3

4
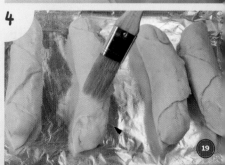

19

DELICIOUS
Sausage Pita

You'll be a hero for making this gyro!

INGREDIENTS

1 cucumber, diced
½ cup plain Greek yogurt
½ cup sour cream
2 tablespoons chopped red onion
1 teaspoon garlic, minced
1 tablespoon lemon juice
1 teaspoon salt
½ tablespoon rice vinegar

1 tablespoon olive oil
6 sausages, chopped
8 pita rounds
4 cups chopped lettuce
1 tomato, chopped
½ cup crumbled feta cheese

TOOLS

sharp knife
cutting board
measuring cups
measuring spoons
mixing bowl
mixing spoon
saucepan
pot holders

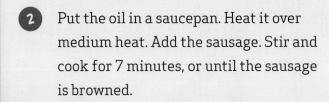

1 Put the cucumber, yogurt, sour cream, onion, garlic, lemon juice, salt, and rice vinegar in a bowl. Stir them together.

2 Put the oil in a saucepan. Heat it over medium heat. Add the sausage. Stir and cook for 7 minutes, or until the sausage is browned.

3 Add the sausage to the cucumber mixture. Stir them together.

4 Put some of the sausage mixture on each pita.

5 Add lettuce and tomato to each pita. Sprinkle feta cheese on top of each pita.

1

4

5

WHITE BEAN & Sausage Pasta

You'll love every bite!

INGREDIENTS

6 ounces penne pasta

¼ cup pine nuts

1 tablespoon olive oil

1 package smoked sausage, sliced

1 zucchini, sliced

½ cup chicken stock

3 cups broccoli florets

1 15-ounce can white beans, drained and rinsed

1 cup sliced cherry tomatoes

TOOLS

measuring cups

measuring spoons

sharp knife

cutting board

large pot

colander

rubber spatula

mixing bowls

mixing spoon

pot holders

1 Cook the pasta according to the directions on the package. Drain the pasta.

2 Put the pine nuts in a large pot over medium heat. Stir and cook for about 3 minutes. Put the pine nuts in a bowl.

3 Put the olive oil and sausage in the pot over medium heat. Stir and cook for 5 minutes. Add them to the pine nuts.

4 Put the zucchini and chicken stock in the pot over medium heat. Cook for 5 minutes. Add the broccoli, beans, and tomatoes. Cook for 2 minutes.

5 Turn the heat to low. Add the pasta, sausage, and pine nuts. Stir and cook for 1 minute.

SPICY
Sausage Stir Fry

Stir up a stunning meal!

INGREDIENTS

2 tablespoons olive oil
4 precooked sausages
1 tablespoon minced garlic
1½ cups broccoli florets
1 green bell pepper, sliced
1 red bell pepper, sliced
1 orange bell pepper, sliced

½ cup green beans
2 tablespoons soy sauce
1 tablespoon
   Worcestershire sauce

TOOLS

measuring spoons
measuring cups
sharp knife
cutting board
large pot
mixing spoon
pot holders

1 Put 1 tablespoon of olive oil in a large pot. Heat it over medium heat. Add the sausages. Cook for 5 to 6 minutes. Break up the sausages with a spoon. Take the sausage out of the pot.

2 Put the garlic, broccoli, peppers, beans, and the rest of the olive oil in the pot. Cook for 4 minutes over medium heat.

3 Stir in the soy sauce and the Worcestershire sauce.

4 Add the sausage. Stir and cook for 5 minutes.

1

3

4

SAVORY
Sausage Soup

This soup will warm you up!

2 tablespoons olive oil

8 smoked turkey sausages, cut into 1-inch (2.5 cm) slices

1 cup chopped onions

3 garlic cloves, minced

½ cup sliced carrots

3 tomatoes, diced

2 teaspoons thyme

6 cups chicken stock

2 15-ounce cans white beans, drained and rinsed

8 ounces spinach leaves

¼ teaspoon cayenne pepper

measuring spoons

sharp knife

cutting board

measuring cups

large pot

mixing spoon

colander

pot holders

1 Put the oil and sausages in a large pot. Stir and cook over medium heat for 4 minutes.

2 Add the onions, garlic, and carrots. Stir and cook for about 10 minutes.

3 Add the tomatoes, thyme, chicken stock, and beans. Bring the soup to a boil. Turn the heat down to low. Simmer for 25 minutes.

4 Stir in the spinach and the cayenne pepper. Cook for 5 minutes.

1

3

4

SAUSAGE & Apple Salad

28

SALAD

2 apple chicken sausage
links, sliced

1 tablespoon olive oil

1 green apple, sliced

½ tablespoon lemon juice

4 cups mixed greens

¼ cup crumbled feta cheese

⅓ cup chopped walnuts

DRESSING

¼ cup mayonnaise

1 tablespoon mustard

1 tablespoon honey

½ tablespoon white
vinegar

sharp knife

cutting board

measuring
spoons

measuring
cups

medium
saucepan

mixing spoon

pot holders

mixing bowls

whisk

2 forks

4 salad plates

1   Put the sausage and oil in a saucepan.
Cook over medium heat for 5 minutes.
Let the sausages cool.

2   Put the apple slices and lemon juice
in a bowl. Stir to coat the apples with
the juice.

3   Put the dressing ingredients in a small
bowl. Whisk them together.

4   Put the mixed greens and the dressing
in a large bowl. Toss to coat the greens
with dressing.

5   Put some of the greens on each salad
plate. Arrange apple slices and sausage
on each salad. Sprinkle cheese and
walnuts on top.

1

4

5

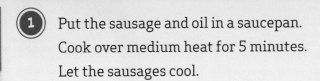

Conclusion

Explore the world
of sausage dishes.
What else can
you cook up?

Main dishes are fun to make and share! Feel proud of the dishes you prepare. Eat them with your family and friends. Sausage is one of many great ingredients for main dishes. Don't stop with sausage. Try other ingredients too!

Glossary

dessert – a sweet food, such as fruit, ice cream, or pastry, served after a meal.

diagonally – from one corner of a square to the opposite corner.

gyro – a Greek sandwich on pita bread that includes meat, tomato, onion, and yogurt sauce.

patty – a round, flat cake made with chopped or ground food.

permission – when a person in charge says it's okay to do something.

pork – meat that comes from a pig.

thaw – to melt or unfreeze.

towel – a cloth or paper used for cleaning or drying.

utensil – a tool used to prepare or eat food.

WEBSITES

To learn more about Cool Main Dishes, visit **booklinks.abdopublishing.com**. These links are routinely monitored and updated to provide the most current information available.

Index